Pixels Are the New Ink:

Three steps to digital domination in your industry

Jeff Tippett

Table of Contents

Introduction

Every day, you're leaving money on the table – and your competitors are raking it up.

Is it because they're smarter than you, or work harder? Probably not.

Their advantage is that they've found a way to take their product or service directly to their audience with precision, and are doing it extremely well. They've learned secrets for targeting their clients and customers in a cost-effective manner. They're no longer seeking the masses: They're targeting their clients – online.

You see, the days of seeking ink from newspapers to build your brand are long over. You don't need traditional media to dominate your industry. You now have the ability to build your personal brand – online. You *can* take charge of your destiny. The problem is that most people don't know how to do this, or at least how to do it well.

First, a disclaimer:

This book is not designed to be an exhaustive look into building your online profile. Rather, it's designed to introduce you to the three pillars necessary to dominate your industry. From this launching point, I hope you'll dig deeper, and have fun!

I believe we've reached the point of no return with social media: It's no longer an option. If you want to be relevant in today's marketplace, you have to build an online presence. If you're the type that's still questioning or pushing back on the value of online, there's no need to waste your time reading this book. But if you're at least curious about building your online presence, this book is perfect for you.

Building your online presence isn't about mass; it's about niche. I think of people like Grant Cardone, Jordan Harbinger and Lewis Howes. If you're part of their target market, you've either heard of them or you're about to. They have successfully built niche markets that are growing every single day. They understand how to dive deep with the right audience. What's the value in pushing your brand to a mass group when there's no likely conversion or return on your investment?

Let me add a word of caution:

This approach isn't for those who are seeking a quick fix. If you think you'll instantly become famous, making tons of money, you can stop reading now. But if you have stamina, are willing to roll up your sleeves and work hard and are prepared to see this through to the long game – keep reading.

Now that those not willing to do the work have abandoned this book, let me offer this assurance for those of you remaining: This isn't complicated. There's a simple formula for becoming a digital rockstar, those three pillars of digital success: produce and distribute content, build your audience and engage.

Yes, it's that simple.

In the following pages, I'm going to show you how you can put more money in the bank by dominating your industry in the digital space. The landscape has changed. It's a new game. Old systems are collapsing. But those who have vision and are smart enough to embrace digital marketing will dominate their market. And I want that person to be you.

Before we move ahead, allow me to make one assurance:

You may be wondering if this book is for you. Perhaps you're a CEO or other executive within a company, an entrepreneur, an activist or the executive director of an association or nonprofit. Or maybe you're stuck in your current job, have a dream and want to find your way to starting your own company.

Regardless of your title or lack thereof, if you have a message to share (and we all have a message), if you have passion to do something great with your life, if you're willing to put in the work and the idea of depositing money in the bank appeals to you – this book is for you. That's right: I've written this book just for you!

Why wait? Let's get started now!

Part 1:

Produce and Distribute Content

Becoming a digital rockstar begins with producing content and distributing it. Now, the type of content will vary depending on multiple factors: your product, your audience, the time you have available. But first you need to get your expertise out of your head and share it with others.

Before you strike the first key on your tablet or laptop to begin writing content, take a pause. There are two areas I want you to think through before you launch your quest to dominate online.

Always start with your goals. Ask yourself, "What am I trying to accomplish?" You'll save a lot of wasted time if you begin with where you want to go. While these goals may shift over time, you need to remain focused on where you want to arrive.

Understand you. Prior to starting out, you need to figure out *you*. Nilofer Merchant calls this *onlyness*, which she defines this way:

"Onlyness is that thing that only that one individual can bring to a situation. It includes the journey and passions of each human.

Onlyness is fundamentally about honoring each person: first as we view ourselves and second as we are valued. Each of us is standing in a spot that no one else occupies. That unique point of view is born of our accumulated experience, perspective, and vision. Some of those experiences are not as 'perfect' as we might want, but even those experiences are a source for what you create."

I sincerely encourage you to read through Merchant's work. Judy Carter's book *The Message of You* is another highly recommended resource. Think through your onlyness. If you can't state your onlyness, you will never stand out in the crowded sea of online marketing.

Find your voice. Ever listen to Gary V or Grant Cardone? They have distinct voices. Your tone sets you apart from everyone else in this crowded field; it builds trust and helps determine how you'll persuade.

Finding your voice will come over time. But you need to start where you are and allow your voice to reveal itself through your work. Then, once you understand your voice, I encourage you to keep it consistent. Be you. You'll discover your unique ways for communicating ideas to your audience.

Produce the Right Content

Did you catch that? This is about producing the *right* content. The web – more specifically, social media – is inundated with content. Every day, millions of people post things that really have no value. So how do you produce content that stands out?

Here's how to begin:

Determine the problem you intend to solve. Your target market has problems. Basically, the concept is this: People will pay for solutions to their problems. What solutions do you bring to the table? Focus on your audience's needs, and they'll pay attention to you – then hire you to help!

Don't be boring. Boring content is everywhere, and an audience is easily lost. You need to capture their attention quickly. Stand out by using shocking quotes, saying something unusual, evoking emotions. Ernest Hemingway said, "Write drunk; edit sober."

The Time I Almost Stole a Bathrobe from the Omni Hotel

While staying at the Omni Hotel in downtown Atlanta for a business conference, I noticed a nice white, lightweight, branded bathrobe in my closet. I'm not sure why, but it caught my attention, and I thought it would look better hanging in my closet at home.

Without a lot of thought, I snapped a quick pic as I was heading to the elevator to go out for a run. I posted the pic on Twitter with a short message about how much I liked the robe in my Omni hotel room, and added that I might "borrow" it. I'd no sooner walked off the elevator than I received a tweet back from Omni Hotels! The hotel indicated they were glad I liked it and asserted that instead of borrowing it, I was welcomed to buy one in the gift shop.

My tweet didn't include Omni's twitter handle. It merely had the word "Omni" in it. Omni was monitoring the word "Omni." The pic was viewed thousands of times, lots of people commented, and I praised Omni Hotels for paying attention online, engaging in the conversation and making the exchanges fun. This conversation lasted all day!

After a full night exploring Atlanta, I returned to my hotel room to an unexpected surprise.

Within seconds of opening the door, I noticed my desk lamp was on, and there was a present. The kid in me took over and I rushed to see what it was.

Omni Hotels had capped off a great day of online conversation by leaving one of the coveted robes as a gift. And they included a handwritten note thanking me for the full day promoting their brand. Although I wouldn't have actually "borrowed" the robe, I broke through the online noise with a fun tweet. And Omni Hotels engaged with (or indulged) me. The result was increased brand awareness – in a positive way.

And it all started with a post that apparently wasn't boring.

Create content your niche market needs. Think back to my first point, about solving the problem, then predict your audience's pressure points. Speak to those. Be a trusted resource to your target audience. Then you can lead.

"The art of communication is the language of leadership."
– James Humes

Provide value. People need your expertise. You have to have the mindset that you're the expert. You have knowledge that your audience needs. Ask yourself, "What knowledge do I have that others need?" If you provide value, they'll eat up your content, and they'll be loyal followers. Make sure you message in a way that people can understand, and that you give them actionable steps to solve their problem.

"The difference between the right word and the almost right word is the difference between lightning and lightning bug."
– Mark Twain

Focus on effective communication. I believe we all experience information overload. Think about how much information is given out daily through seminars, TV, radio, social media, etc. Everywhere we turn, we're bombarded with information.

But there's a market for your expertise if you focus on communication. What's the difference? Sydney J. Harris explains the difference between information and communication this way: "The two words 'information' and 'communication' are used interchangeably, but they signify quite different things. Information is giving out; communication is getting through."

Always choose authenticity. Your users want

to know and trust you. I think we sometimes forget that we're communicating with other human beings. While listening to one of my favorite podcasters today, he mentioned being sexually abused as a child. This guy has one of the largest, most successful podcasts dealing with business issues. And he mentioned being sexually abused. I instantly related and felt a strong bond with him. I understand it sounds strange to think of bonding with a person through digital media, but it's possible. And being authentic with your audience will build loyalty.

Be passionate. If you want to rise to the top quickly, speak to your passions. Show the fire that's inside you. Don't be afraid to sound fanatical about your subject matter. There are plenty of boring communicators, and you'll likely never gain traction online if you aren't passionate. You want to move people to action, and your passion can drive that action.

"Effective communication is 20% what you know and 80% how you feel about what you know."
– Jim Rohn

Tell stories. Want to drive home your point quickly, and in a memorable, sticky manner? Tell a story. Most likely, those consuming your content will forget the facts. But they will remember the truth they learned in your stories. Keep those stories interesting and fun. Humor is your friend!

Good and now is better than perfect and tomorrow. If you're a perfectionist, this is hard to accept. Too often, demanding perfection stalls your ability to move forward now and causes you to miss opportunities.

"The ultimate pitch for an era of short attention spans begins with a single word – and doesn't go any further."
– Daniel Pink

Distribute Content

So you now understand how to create the *right* content. Now what do you do with it? You have to determine what platform(s) you'll use to get it out to the public. In determining what communications platforms to use, ask this question: "Where is my target market?" That's where you want to be.

But before you push out your first piece of content, I want you to commit to consistently showing up. You have to be in the conversation, all the time. This is one reason I love and use scheduled and automated posts. Don't go ghost on your audience. Show up with regular frequency. No matter what.

With that commitment, you're ready to start sharing content. Here's how to do it.

Post an article. This article can be posted on your blog. If you don't have a blog, no worries. There are sites like medium.com where you can set up an account in less than two minutes and begin publishing. You can also write a post on LinkedIn or your other existing social sites.

Post a video. Now, I realize creating a video seems intimidating to a lot of people. You want quality that represents your brand well. Producing videos can be expensive, but it doesn't have to be. In fact, your videos will probably gain more traction if they're less polished and more authentic. I encourage you to consider them.

Record a podcast. You may well find that your target market consumes podcasts. I'm one of those people. Almost every time I'm in my car, I have a podcast playing. If you decide to move forward with podcasting, check out Clammr for converting lengthy podcasts into short sound bites for sharing on social media.

Broadcast a live event. Facebook LIVE is currently gaining a lot of traction. It's a quick, easy way to test messaging – to explore new ideas, see how people respond and make decisions about building out the content. Why not give it a try?

Share on social media. Hands down, social media is the largest driver of traffic to my website. And Twitter champions all my social networks. I realize that social media can be time consuming, and often people question the return on investment. Since I know it brings value but I have limited time, I use Hootsuite's Bulk Uploader. In just a few hours a month, I can upload all my social posts; I determine the distribution time. Another great resource is Edgar. If you're heavy into Pinterest, try scheduling with Tailwind. Or Grum, Kistagram or Onlypult for Instagram. And Facebook has a built-in scheduler.

Keep in mind that you should always include an image with your posts. I often use branded personal images. You may want to select a stunning, relevant image from a service such as Over, Quick, Typorama or Enlight. You can add captions instantly from your mobile. And if your target is into Instagram, create a beautiful image with a striking headline. Also, consider using sponsored posts in Facebook if you determine it's worth the investment.

Brand your short links when sharing on social media. Since your links have to be shortened, why promote Bitly or TinyURL? My links are all shortened with my name. My current favorite is short.cm. Links look like this: http://jefftippett.co/inKUqx. You can also track conversion rates using this service.

Tweeting for a Decade

I joined Twitter in October 2007. It's hard to believe that as I write this book, I'm approaching a decade of tweeting. I'm approaching 50,000 tweets!

When I first began tweeting, people laughed – and that was after I had to explain what 'tweeting' was. I heard comments like:

"What a waste of time."
"That'll disappear soon."
"Why are you doing this?"

In the early days, there was a period when Twitter was down on what seemed a daily basis. So most of my friends moved to a service called Plurk.

I remember the first area-wide "tweetup." This event was a face-to-face gathering of people who had only been talking online. Boy, was that weird.

But Twitter has remained a staple of my online communication. Why?

- *It's my number-one driver of website traffic.*
- *I can catch people's attention like on no other platform.*
- *I can test messaging.*
- *I can exhibit thought leadership.*
- *I can meet interesting people.*
- *I've won contests.*
- *And so much more!*

When I was planning a town hall in support of short-term rentals like Airbnb, I casually tweeted that I was working on the event. My plan was to send out a media alert the next day. But within 30 minutes of my tweet, I was on the phone with my local newspaper and they were asking for details. All from a single tweet!

But you'll have to figure out value for yourself. Test the type of content, frequency, time, etc. You'll find what works for you and create solid engagement with your followers.

Send an email. While some marketers are claiming that email marketing is dead, it's not. Email marketing is one of the fastest and most cost-effective ways to engage your audience. As long as you're providing content of value, people will likely welcome your emails. I encourage you to use an email service that will allow you to test things like subject lines and delivery times. You'll also want to pay attention to open rates and click-through rates to better understand what's working for your audience. And I would encourage you to offer for people to opt in to your email marketing every opportunity you get.

I'm often asked how frequently to send emails. And the answer is simple yet complicated: it depends. There are a few questions to think through to help you make your best guess, and then you should test. We understand that it takes frequency to build a brand. We also understand that getting spammed with junk email is annoying. So how do you make your best guess?

I think the number-one driver for the frequency of email delivery is the nature of your content. Is it bringing value? Is there a timing issue for your content to consider? Are you breaking news? What, exactly, are you providing?

Every morning I wake to two emails that I love, and both are from *The New York Times*: Today's Headlines and Your (Insert day of week) Briefing. In less than 60 seconds, I feel that I have at least a high-level awareness of important news. I value this content because I use it every day in conversations. It brings value, and the information is time sensitive. So I look forward to reading (or perusing) these emails. On the other hand, yesterday I unsubscribed from an email campaign that was being sent once a month. Why? There was no value.

I encourage you to make your best guess. Then test. Try different frequencies of distribution, times of distribution, subject lines, content placement, colors, etc. Your audience will tell you everything you need to know.

Repurpose content. How about this: Write an article; share on your blog, Medium, and LinkedIn; distribute the article via email using a platform like MailChimp; produce a quick video and put a link to your article in the description and upload to YouTube or Wistia; take the audio and upload to Sticher; then create a striking image with a headline that makes people click, and add a link in the description and share on Instagram and Facebook.

Whew! That's a lot.

But here's my point: If you're going to take the time to generate content, why not maximize that asset by sharing on as many platforms as possible? Now, the qualifier is making sure your market is on that platform. But if they are, fire away! Why is this technique important to your success? Most likely, a potential client won't respond immediately. It takes multiple impressions to capture their attention. So maximize your assets.

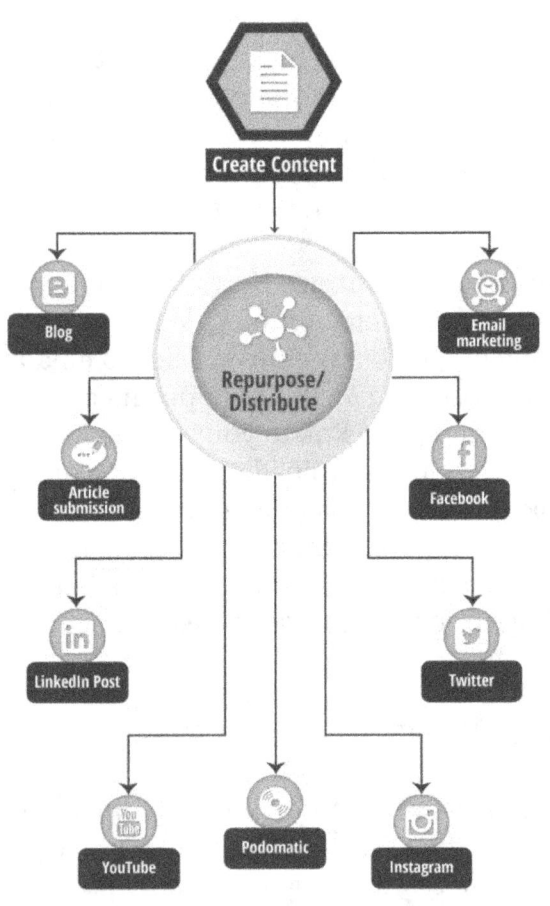

Repost the same content. You should promote the same content multiple times, but with unique messaging. Post lifecycles on social media are short. In fact, a tweet has a shelf life of 18 minutes or less. So I'll push users to my online content using tons of different posts. Be careful not to be overly blatant in self-promotion; mix in outside content that will bring value to your followers.

Share the same content at various times and with various messaging. And remember to test to find out what works for you. There's so much in the sales process that depends on your potential client's timing. You have to be there when the time is right. So keep the content flowing. When they're ready to pay for a solution to their problem, you have to be right there in front of them with the solution.

In his book *The Respect Effect*, Paul Meshanko explains why reposting is so important as he describes a successful ad campaign:

"No matter how compelling the message, if it's played only once or twice, there's very little chance of it influencing perceptions and intentions strongly enough to result in the desired buyer behaviors."

You need repetition of your messaging. Repost the same content (but in unique ways), and watch your messaging start to take hold with your audience. Conversely, say it only once, and you'll likely be disappointed with the results.

Autoscheduling. As I mentioned, the majority of my online posts are scheduled in advance; I autoschedule about once a month. I fill in with daily posts of things happening in the moment, but the main structure of my social media posts is planned well in advance. For me, it's an efficient way to be active on social media. In three or four hours a month, I can bulk upload posts to Twitter, Facebook, LinkedIn and Google+. This is the system that works for me. Take a look at the bulk uploaded feature of Hootsuite, Buffer or Edgar. Or find the product that works best for you.

Autopost trusted content. To maintain a balance of self-promotion and promotion of others', I use MarketHub. This service allows me to choose selected sources, and it then autoposts to Twitter when these trusted sources have new content. This service is worth the price.

Pitch to online influencers. Want to catapult your brand awareness at warp speed? Pitch your content to online influencers. Perhaps they'll interview you on their podcast or video channel, include your ideas in their next blog post and credit you or share on Facebook. If you've developed top-notch content, reach out to online influencers whose audiences will find your content of value. And get ready for a lot of online hits!

Test messaging and platforms. What messaging works? What messaging doesn't work? Which platforms are delivering a solid return? Focus on where the return is. You can't be everything to everyone and be everywhere. Testing will provide you the answers.

Jeff Tippett @JeffTippett · Feb 16
Is your company intentionally doing good? You should. Here's why.
jefftippett.co/inKUqx

This @jefftippett post on Twitter shows the branded link shortener and branded image.

Part 2

Build Your Audience

Have you heard this philosophical question before? If a tree falls in the forest and nobody's there to hear it, does it make a sound?

The answer is "no."

Why no? Because sound comprises three parts: initiation, transmission medium and receiver. Sound is the sensation excited in the ear when the air or another medium is set in motion.

You can produce content all day long. Distribute it all night long. But if you don't have an audience, of what value is it? It's of no value, and you've wasted your time. The "if you build it, they will come" mantra just doesn't work when building your online audience.

"Content is king, distribution is queen, and she wears the pants."
– Jonathan Perelman, VP Agency Strategy, BuzzFeed

You've now committed to producing and distributing content. Now it's time to build your targeted audience so that your message has a place to land.

How do you do it?

Add your social links – everywhere. Promoting your social media has to constantly be top of mind. Think of all the places your audience is already seeing you. For example:

- Email signature
- Presentation slides
- Handouts
- Personalized note cards

Cross-promote on your social channels. Most likely, people that follow you on a social network are also on other networks. If you're already connected on one network, why not encourage them to follow you on other networks too? Anything you can do to increase your brand awareness and offer additional ways to engage will bring value to you as you digitally dominate your industry. Remember: You need frequency of brand exposure.

Paid social traffic. One solid way to increase brand awareness and engagement and gain new followers is to pay for sponsored posts. Three important caveats here:

1. Make sure the content is solid and brings recognized value.
2. Target your posts (geography, interests, demographics, etc.).
3. Use retargeting to keep your message in front of people who have already engaged.

Follow your target market. They will likely follow you back. Use Twitter search to find the people and potential hashtags. And you can always experiment with services like Instagress for Instagram that autofollow.

Use hashtags. When you're attending a conference, sitting in on a presentation or following a news story, add smart comments and include hashtags. People who are following the conversation through hashtags are likely part of your desired audience. By using the hashtag, others at the gathering can find you. But you can also be aggressive and engage people who've used the hashtag. Try adding a well-thought-out response to their post. Say something unique. Stand out. If they like you and find value, they're likely to follow you online. And consider following them.

A hashtag is a keyword or phrase preceded by the hash symbol (#) that people include in their social media posts. It makes the content of your post accessible to all people with similar interests, even if they're not your followers or fans.

Hijack influencers. Who are the top influencers in your vertical? Who has a large, engaged network? Build a list and find these influencers online. Then generate some content. Maybe write an article or shoot a video expanding on a topic they mention. Make sure that whatever you generate brings value. Now it's showtime! Hit them up on social media. Make your message intriguing. Then watch! Most likely they'll respond, allowing their followers to be exposed to your brand.

I Wanted A Response. I Wasn't Disappointed.

I recently listened to a podcast from Art of Charm in which Jordan Harbinger was interviewing Jocelyn Glei. The podcast spoke to me at a time when I really needed the message. And it inspired me to write an article for my website. So I shared the article on Twitter and tagged Harbinger and Glei. As expected, they responded! Here's the exchange:

↩ In reply to Jeff Tippett

Jordan Harbinger ✔ @T... · 1/29/17 ⌄
@JeffTippett @jkglei thanks Jeff!
Glad you got so much out of this!
What other episodes of AoC really
hit lately?

Share content in groups on Facebook and LinkedIn. I highly encourage you to join groups in social media that are relevant to your market. Be a regular contributor, but mix in content from others. And please don't spam the group with unwanted, irrelevant self-promotion.

Comment on Facebook and LinkedIn posts. You're smart; you're an industry expert. All this great knowledge is in your head, and you need to get it out. If you're going to take the time to read a post of value in LinkedIn or Facebook, why not add a quick but well-thought-out comment? You'll gain exposure with people you're likely trying to reach. And it'll probably only take a minute or two. You'll find it's a small effort with a solid return.

Part 3

Engage

You've got a firm handle on creating and distributing the right content and you've built a solid audience. So what else does it take to make you the digital expert in your field? You have to engage in the online conversation.

How do you do this?

Listen. Of all the points I'll make in this section, none is more important than this one. Listening is an often-neglected skill in our society. And it's the number-one way you can let a person know that you care. There's plenty of time to share your vast knowledge. Slow down and listen first. As Jeff Daly says, "Two monologues do not make a dialogue."

Be social. Social media is, obviously, meant to be social. It's not about you constantly posting messages about yourself. You must engage in others' conversations. Think about it: How would it be if you went to a networking event and spoke only of yourself, never asked questions of others, went from group to group only talking about *you*? Yeah, that wouldn't go over so well, would it?

Be consistent with your voice. Every single post and every single response is part of how you're building your brand. You're developing your voice. It takes frequency and consistency to establish this brand. One foul comment or post could bring serious damage to your brand. Unfortunately, we've entered an era in which being rude online is quickly becoming a norm. Don't get drug into that.

Share others' content. One way to instantly make online friends is to share their content. When you notice a post that you think will bring value to your audience, share it. But take it one step further: Add smart commentary. This will accomplish three things: (1) you'll have additional content of value for your audience, (2) you'll earn good will with the person that originally posted the message and (3) that original poster will see how smart you are with the added commentary. It's a formula for success all around. Besides, constant self-promotion will get tuned out. If you share the gems of others much more frequently than your own, your gems will start to stand out.

Add smart comments. If you're taking the time to read tweets, Facebook/LinkedIn posts or blogs, why not take a quick minute to add a smart comment? It doesn't have to be a thesis – just a quick observation is all you need. You'll raise your brand awareness with everyone who read the post and comment.

Tag or mention others. When appropriate, tag or mention people in your post. For example, if you've written an article that includes another brand, tag that brand in Twitter as you share. There's a good chance that the brand you mentioned will engage in the conversation. And now you've increased your credibility and exposure. Find people with massive online followings and hijack their network. Ask them a question, share your content with them or find some reason to get them to respond to you. You'll expand your exposure to their networks.

Keep the conversation going. Once you've engaged in an online conversation, keep it going by asking a clarifying question or even asking the person to take a next step. Lewis Howes (@LewisHowes) is the master of this strategy. Since he's an industry expert, I tweeted him with a comment. Notice how he continues the conversation by asking for a review. Brilliant.

↰ In reply to Jeff Tippett

Lewis Howes ✓ @LewisH... · 1/31/17 ⌄
@JeffTippett @TheArtofCharm
thanks! And would love a review if
you have a moment! iTunes.com/
schoolofgreatn...

Conclusion

When it comes to digital media, I often say that nothing has changed while everything has changed. The platforms, frequencies of engagement and tools have changed dramatically. But at the core of communicating as a human being, all the same rules apply. Respect others. Respond when people mention you. Initiate conversations.

See what I mean? While the platforms and pace of conversations have changed, all the manners you learned in kindergarten need to remain in place.

You create and distribute content, you build your audience and you engage. This formula is simple and foolproof. But you have to consistently work the formula, focusing on all three legs of the stool. Without all three components, your stool will collapse.

Have fun. Be creative. Be successful. And share your success with me.

Congratulations! You made it to the end. If you're like other readers, you're ready for the next step: creating your detailed, concrete plan to building your digital empire. So, here's your opportunity for me to help you!

Visit
PixelsAreTheNewInk.com

For tools to dig deeper into the concepts presented in this book. I want to help you win!